Indigenous Celebrations

Ian Rohr

A+

Smart Apple Media
P.O. Box 3263
Mankato, MN, 56002

First published in 2010 by
MACMILLAN EDUCATION AUSTRALIA PTY LTD
15–19 Claremont St, South Yarra, Australia 3141

Visit our web site at www.macmillan.com.au or go directly to www.macmillanlibrary.com.au

Associated companies and representatives throughout the world.

Library of Congress Cataloging-in-Publication Data

Rohr, Ian.
  Indigenous celebrations / Ian Rohr.
    p. cm. -- (Celebrations around the world)
  Includes index.
  ISBN 978-1-59920-537-3 (library binding)
  1. Festivals--Cross-cultural studies--Juvenile literature. 2. Indigenous peoples--Social life and customs--Juvenile literature. I.
Title.
  GT3933.R632 2011
  394.26--dc22

                          2009042142

Publisher: Carmel Heron
Managing Editor: Vanessa Lanaway
Editor: Michaela Forster
Proofreader: Kirstie Innes-Will
Designer: Kerri Wilson (cover and text)
Page layout: Pier Vido
Photo researcher: Wendy Duncan
Production Controller: Vanessa Johnson

Manufactured in China by Macmillan Production (Asia) Ltd.
Kwun Tong, Kowloon, Hong Kong
Supplier Code: CP January 2010

6117

Acknowledgments
The author and the publisher are grateful to the following for permission to reproduce copyright material:

Cover photograph: Children doing a 'Purlapa' traditional dance in the Warlpiri Aboriginal community in the Northern Territory, Australia, © Ludo Kuipers/APL/Corbis

AAP Image/Sakchai Lalit, 13; © Yann Arthus-Bertrand/Corbis, 28; © Richard A. Cooke/Corbis, 29; © Ed Kashi/Corbis, 19; © Ludo Kuipers/APL/Corbis, 1, 9; Full Circle: First Nations Performance/Chris Randle, 20, 21; © Rich Legg/iStockphoto, 4; © Jupiter Unlimited/Thinkstock Images, 5; © Sylvain Grandadam/The Image Bank/Getty Images, 25; © Michael Langford/ Gallo Images/Getty Images, 22, 23; © Frederic Pacorel/Workbook Stock/Getty Images, 12; © Selwyn Tait/Time & Life Pictures/Getty Images, 24; © Penny Tweedie/The Image Bank/Getty Images, 6; © Marilyn Angel Wynn/Nativestock.com/Getty Images, 7; Newspix/Peter Clark, 15; Newspix/Alita Pashley, 14; photolibrary/Daniel Hurst, 18; photolibrary/Mary Evans Picture Library, 8; Reuters/David Mercado, 11; © Shutterstock/Kevin Renes, 30; © UN Photo/Paulo Filgueiras, 10; © Wairoa Maori Film Festival/ Leo Koziol, 26, 27; © Yothu Yindi Foundation, 16, 17.

While every care has been taken to trace and acknowledge copyright, the publisher tenders their apologies for any accidental infringement where copyright has proved untraceable. Where the attempt has been unsuccessful, the publisher welcomes information that would redress the situation.

Contents

When a word is printed in **bold**, you can look up its meaning in the Glossary on page 31.

Celebrations

Celebrations are events that are held on special occasions. Some are events from the past that are still celebrated. Others celebrate important times in our lives or activities, such as music.

Birthdays are special events that many people celebrate.

Some celebrations involve only a few people.
Others involve whole cities or countries.
Large celebrations take place across the world.

New Year's Eve is celebrated all around
the world with fireworks.

What Are Indigenous Celebrations?

Indigenous people are the first people to live in a country or region. Indigenous celebrations are events that celebrate the **culture** and **traditions** of indigenous people.

Many indigenous Australians celebrate ways of life that are thousands of years old.

Indigenous celebrations often use stories, songs, and **ceremonies**. These have been passed from older people to younger people over time.

Indigenous people from Canada and the United States perform ceremonies that have been passed down over many years.

Indigenous Celebrations in the Past

Many indigenous celebrations have been held for thousands of years. Some are religious celebrations. Others celebrate the **harvest** or the coming of spring.

Old pictures show how some indigenous people celebrated in the past.

Many indigenous celebrations stopped when new **settlers** brought their own ways of celebrating. Now, many indigenous people perform their own celebrations again. This keeps their culture alive.

Indigenous celebrations can help young people learn about their history.

International Day of the World's Indigenous People

The International Day of the World's Indigenous People is held on August 9 every year. The **United Nations** meets to celebrate indigenous people from around the world.

Performances by indigenous people at the United Nations meeting are part of the celebration.

The aim of this day is to improve the lives of the world's indigenous people. This involves many events and activities.

Some indigenous people hold **ceremonies** on the International Day of the World's Indigenous People.

Tadua Kaamatan, Malaysia

Tadua Kaamatan is a harvest festival. It is held by the indigenous people of Sabah in Malaysia. Tadua Kaamatan takes place at the end of May every year.

Tadua Kaamatan celebrates the end of the rice harvest.

Tadua Kaamatan is celebrated with music and dancing. Traditional food and drink are also part of the celebrations, along with games and sports.

Buffalo racing is one of the events held at Tadua Kaamatan.

NAIDOC Week, Australia

NAIDOC Week celebrates Australia's indigenous people. It takes place every year in July. All Australians are encouraged to celebrate NAIDOC Week.

Some indigenous Australians march through the streets during NAIDOC Week.

Each year, NAIDOC Week has a special **theme**.
A different Australian city hosts a big celebration,
called a ball. At the ball, special **awards**
are presented.

NAIDOC Week celebrations include indigenous
dance performances.

Garma Festival, Australia

Garma Festival celebrates the Yolngu (say *Yol-ng-oo*) people of northeast Arnhem Land in Australia. The Yolngu have lived there for more than 40,000 years.

People come from all over Australia to celebrate Garma Festival.

Garma Festival is held in early August each year. It celebrates the Yolngu's way of living. Songs and ceremonies keep their traditions alive.

The Yolngu perform traditional dances at Garma Festival.

American Indian Heritage Month, United States

American Indian Heritage Month celebrates the American Indians of the United States. It takes place during November and involves exhibitions, storytelling, and other activities.

Dance performances are part of American Indian Heritage Month.

During the month, American Indians visit schools to teach children about their culture. They talk about the problems facing the American Indians of the United States.

School children learn about the American Indians of the United States during American Indian Heritage Month.

Talking Stick Festival, Canada

The Talking Stick Festival celebrates the work of the **aboriginal** artists of Canada. It is held each February in Vancouver. Aboriginal artists from all over Canada take part.

The talking stick is a traditional item used in Canadian aboriginal gatherings.

The Talking Stick Festival includes many different types of dance, music, painting, and storytelling. Both famous and new artists take part in the festival.

The children of the Rainbow Drum Group perform at the Talking Stick Festival.

Inti Raymi, Peru and Ecuador

Inti Raymi is a festival held in Peru and Ecuador. Inti Raymi means "festival of the sun" and celebrates the summer. It dates back to the time of the **Incas**.

In Peru, the ruins of Incan buildings are used as a stage for the festival.

For hundreds of years, Spanish settlers did not allow people to celebrate Inti Raymi. Since 1944 it has been celebrated again every year. Inti Raymi includes parades, barbecues, and bonfires.

Parades are an important part of the Inti Raymi festival.

Zindala Zombili, South Africa

Zindala Zombili is one of the largest African festivals. It celebrates the indigenous people of South Africa. Zindala Zombili takes place from April to June.

Many people dress in traditional costumes for the Zindala Zombili festival.

Zindala Zombili celebrations include music and dance. Artists come from across Africa to join in. They put on shows and enter dance and music competitions.

Traditional African dances are an exciting part of Zindala Zombili.

Wairoa Maori and Indigenous Film Festival, New Zealand

The Wairoa Maori and Indigenous Film Festival celebrates films made by the Maori people of New Zealand. It also celebrates films made by indigenous people around the world.

The festival gives prizes to the films voted the best.

The festival takes place in June. Each year the festival has a special theme. Filmmaking workshops are an important part of this festival.

Indigenous filmmakers discuss their films with the audience.

Spring Equinox Festival, Mexico

The Spring **Equinox** Festival celebrates the first day of spring. Mexicans celebrate at the El Castillo **pyramid**. It was built by the **Mayans** more than 500 years ago.

El Castillo is the largest pyramid in Mexico.

At the pyramid, people watch a shadow that looks like a snake. The shadow represents a Mayan snake god. The Mayans believed the shadow was a sign to plant their crops.

Thousands of people gather to watch the snake's shadow move down the El Castillo pyramid.

Try This!

Find the answers to these questions in the book.
(You can check your answers on page 32.)

1. What does the Talking Stick Festival celebrate?
2. When is the International Day of the World's Indigenous People?
3. Where is Inti Raymi celebrated?
4. Who celebrates Tadua Kaamatan?
5. How is Garma Festival celebrated?

Try This Activity

Next time you celebrate a special occasion with your friends or family, ask yourself:

- Why are you celebrating?
- How long have people been celebrating this event?
- Are there other places in the world where people celebrate the event?

30

Glossary

aboriginal	the first people who lived in Canada
awards	prizes given for performing well in a particular area
ceremonies	activities that are performed on special occasions
culture	way of living
equinox	the time of year when day and night are equal lengths
harvest	when the fruits and vegetables on farms are gathered or picked
Incas	the indigenous people of what is now western South America
Mayans	the indigenous people of what is now Mexico
pyramid	a building with a square bottom and sides that come together to form a point
settlers	people who go to live in a new country or place
theme	main idea
traditions	activities and beliefs handed down from older people to younger people
United Nations	an organization many countries belong to
workshops	classes where people are taught skills

Index

Answers to the Quiz on Page 30

1 The work of the aboriginal artists
  of Canada
2 On August 9 each year
3 Peru and Ecuador
4 The indigenous people of Sabah in Malaysia
5 With dances, songs, and ceremonies